SUPER CARRIERS

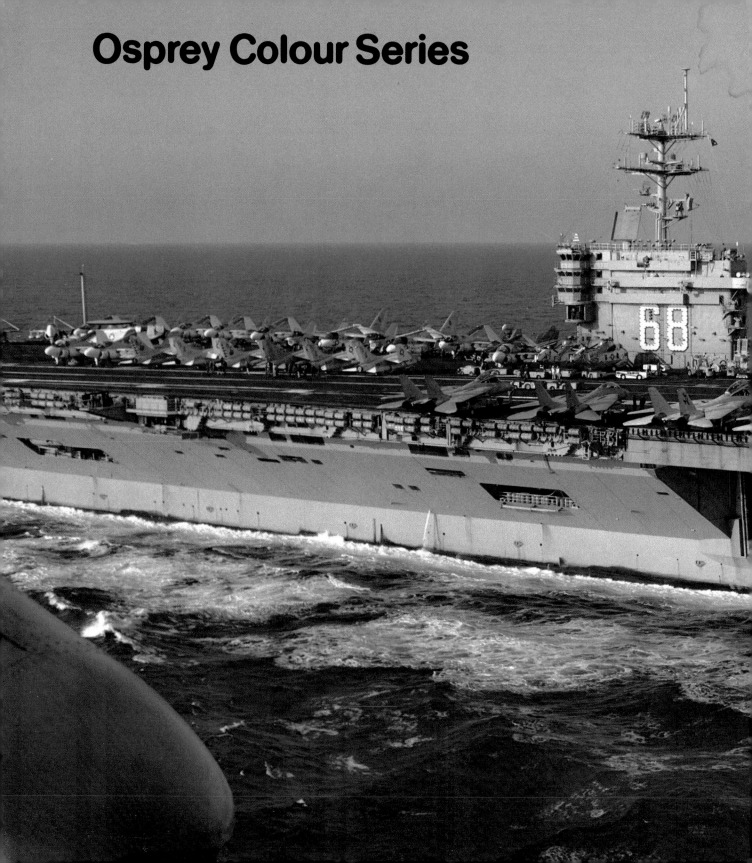

Osprey Colour Series

SUPER CARRIERS

US naval air power today

Jean-Pierre Montbazet

First published in 1985 by Osprey Publishing Limited
27A Floral Street, London WC2E 9DP
Member company of the George Philip Group

Reprinted winter and autumn 1985, 1986

British Library Cataloguing in Publication Data

Montbazet, Jean-Pierre
    Super carriers: US naval air power today.—
    (Osprey Colour Series)
    1. United States. *Navy*—Aviation   2. Airplanes,
    Military—United States
    I. Title
    623.74'6   VG93

ISBN 0-85045-639-8

Editor Dennis Baldry
Designed by Norman Brownsword
Printed in Hong Kong

Front cover A view of flying operations from the
bridge of the USS *Nimitz*: an F-14 Tomcat climbs
away in full 'burner while an S-3A and another
F-14 prepare for launch using the bow catapults

Title pages *Nimitz* steaming at speed through the
Mediterranean, taken from the door of an SH-3H
Sea King helicopter

Back cover Detail of an F-4N Phantom of VF-154
'Black Knights' aboard the USS *Coral Sea* in July
1983

Contents

Jean-Pierre Montbazet is employed as a journalist by the French television station FR3. Aged 35, he lives in Paris with his German-born wife Ingrid and their son, Benjamin. Interestingly, Jean-Pierre met Ingrid in London and they were married in the beautiful English city of Bath in 1976.

The publication of *Super Carriers* is the culmination of Jean-Pierre's enthusiasm for carrier aviation and his extensive programme of visits to the following US Navy aircraft carriers in the Mediterranean Sea: USS *Forrestal* (CV-59), July 1981; *Dwight D. Eisenhower* (CVN-69), June 1982; *Nimitz* (CVN-68), January 1983; *Coral Sea* (CV-43), July 1983; *America* (CV-66), July 1984; and *Saratoga* (CV-60) in August 1984.

This book would not have been possible without the generous help of Captain William A. Rockwell, US naval attaché in Paris, and Philip Brown, Press attaché at the US Embassy in Paris and his staff. The author would also like to thank the United States Navy, the commanders, officers, Press attachés and crews of the CVs for their hospitality and assistance.

Super Carriers was photographed using Nikon cameras and lenses, loaded with Kodak Ektachrome and Kodachrome film.

To my son, Benjamin.

In 1945 the Soviet Navy was little more than a timid coastal defence force. During WW2 it had achieved precisely nothing on the high seas. The United States Navy emerged from global conflict as the world's largest naval power, with battle honours stretching back to the pivotal carrier-versus-carrier showdown off Midway Island in 1942. At the end of the war the US Navy was an unstoppable colossus, spearheaded by literally hundreds of carriers manned by battle-hardened crews and equipped with a galaxy of state-of-the-art naval airplanes.

Forty years later the Soviet Navy is a roving world power with awesome offensive capabilities and, in terms of sheer numbers, is superior to every other navy in the world. But despite the numerical post-war decline of the US Navy and the introduction by the Soviets of 37,000-ton Kiev class air defence carriers (plus one larger nuclear-powered carrier in-build), America looks certain to maintain a clear lead in the building of large carriers, the design of specialized naval aircraft, and the operational procedures and doctrines associated with the use of organic naval air power. By the 1990s the US Navy will be capable of deploying 15 carrier battle groups, including six 93,405-ton Nimitz class nuclear-powered flat-tops.

At the other end of the scale, some carriers operated by smaller navies are best described as floating museums. Other navies have opted to build 'mini-carriers' optimized for V/STOL aircraft: the British Royal Navy commissioned its third and final 19,500-ton Invincible class carrier in July 1985. In the case of France, two nuclear propelled carriers of approximately 35,000 tons are expected to replace *Clemenceau* and *Foch* in the 1990s.

In peacetime the political role of strategic power projection is borne by the US Navy's carrier fleet, but they also train intensively for both conventional and nuclear warfare. If any conflict should break out in Europe, a massive injection of *matériel* from across the Atlantic could make the difference between holding the line and the apocalypse. The intervention of American carrier air power to destroy threats above and below the waves in concert with surface warships and hunter-killer submarines will be a crucial factor in the survival of any task force and, axiomatically, the credibility of further conventional resistance by NATO land forces.

Below KA-6D Intruder of VA-34 'Blue Blasters' parked on the USS *America*.

Top cat

Left VF-103 'Sluggers' use a light gray scheme on their F-14s, but VF-74 'Be-Devilers' prefer overall blue gray. These Tomcats are being readied for flight aboard the USS *Saratoga* (CV-60) in August 1984. **Above** F-14A Tomcat of VF-103 taxies on the flight deck of *Saratoga* before being launched into the sunset. **Overleaf** F-14A Tomcat, side number 201, of VF-103, prepares to launch during inclement Mediterranean weather from one of 'Super Sara's' waist catapults. Its inconspicuous markings and low-profile national insignia blend in with the low visibility paint job

Top left Grumman F-14A Tomcat of VF-41 'Black Aces' on the flight deck of the USS *Nimitz* (CVN-68). The shuttle travelling along the catapult track will be attached to the nosewheel strut of the aircraft. When this procedure is completed, the catapult will be ready to fire. In August 1981, the 'Black Aces' splashed two Libyan Sukhoi Su-22s into the Gulf of Sidra

Overleaf Simultaneous launch of an F-14 and A-7 from the waist and bow catapults of *Nimitz*

Bottom left Directed by a flight deck crewman (identified by his yellow garb) a VF-74 Tomcat lines up for launch from a bow cat on *Saratoga*

Below With a combined total of over 40,000 lb (18,000 kg) of glowing white thrust blasting from the nozzles of its Pratt & Whitney TF30 turbofans, an F-14 is launched from *Saratoga*

Preceding page 'Thumbs-up' from the RIO (radar intercept officer) in the back seat as he and the pilot prepare to withstand the 'kick' of a catapult launch. VF-84 'Jolly Rogers' still wore colourful squadron markings when this picture was taken in January 1983

Left VF-84 Tomcat at the end of the glide path and poised for a perfect touchdown on *Nimitz*. Red-shirted ordnance men know what a good approach looks like—no sign of anything abnormal so no sweat

Below From zero to 160 knots (300 km/h) in 165 ft (50 m): a VF-84 Tomcat sporting the 'skull and crossbones' of the 'Jolly Rogers' clears the bow of *Nimitz*

F-14A Tomcat of VF-41 'Black Aces' successfully engages one of the four arrester cables strung across the deck of *Nimitz*. Take-off thrust is selected at touchdown to ensure that if the pilot lands a little long and misses the wires, or the tailhook hops over them, he has plenty of power to make a safe go-around for another try

F-14A Tomcat, side number 210, of VF-103, launches from *Saratoga*. The Tomcat is probably the best long-range air superiority fighter in the world. It's got so many design features that other combat aircraft look positively austere by comparison.

Tomcat is a Mach 2+, two-seat, twin-engined, twin-finned, variable geometry (with auto-sweep) aircraft with more missile muscle than any other fighter extant. Its combination of Hughes' AWG-9 pulse-Doppler radar and Phoenix/Sparrow/

Sidewinder missiles give it an unrivalled capability against a range of threats; from lightweight fighters to long-range bombers and cruise missiles. Tomcat has successfully destroyed multiple targets at ranges in excess of 100 nm (185 km) with Phoenix missiles. An internal 20 mm M61 Vulcan cannon with 675 rounds is used to hose-down targets at very close range.

Winning the outer air battle (OAB) is what really counts, zapping those bombers *before* they launch nuclear-tipped cruise missiles at the battle group

 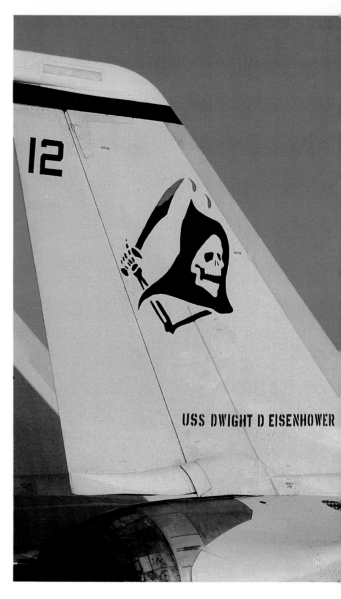

Tomcat tails: VF-33 'Tarsiers'/USS *America*   VF-142 'Ghostriders'/USS *Dwight D. Eisenhower*

VF-74 'Be-Devilers'/USS *Saratoga*

VF-102 'Diamondbacks'/USS *America*

VF-41 Tomcat gets airborne from the *Nimitz*.
Deflector shields are raised to protect men and
machines from the violent heat and blast of each
launch

F-14A Tomcat, side number 214, of VF-103, makes a clean 'trap' aboard *Saratoga* in squally weather. EA-6B fin in foreground displays the bunny motif of VMAQ 2 'Playboys'. The US Navy intends to operate a maximum of 24 Tomcat squadrons and production is expected to pass the 800-mark in the 1990s. A total of 49 F-14s have been modified to carry a centreline TARPS (tactical airborne reconnaissance pod system), and these aircraft have replaced the RA-5C Vigilante and RF-8G Crusader

Two Tomcats of VF-143 'The World Famous Pukin' Dogs' aboard the *Dwight D. Eisenhower*—'IKE'

Right Tomcats of VF-33 (black star) and VF-102 tightly packed on the rear of *America*'s flight deck. The US Navy will begin to take delivery of the upgraded F-14D from 1989. General Electric F110 turbofans each rated at 29,000 lb (13,150 kg) will replace the TF30s, and the new aircraft will also feature the Hornet's AYK-14 central computer, a Honeywell laser-gyro INS (inertial navigation system), multi-function cockpit displays, and a 30 inch (760 mm) fuselage extension to house an additional 2000 lb (907 kg) of fuel. The F-14D will also be fitted with the JTIDS (joint tactical information distribution system) datalink and it's also expected to get a new missile, the AIM-120 AMRAAM

SLUF: the magic war wagon

Left Vought A-7E Corsair II of VA-82 'Marauders' in high visibility markings is ready to taxi to its parking space after being recovered aboard *Nimitz*. The cockpit design of the Corsair bestows its pilot with superb vision in the forward hemisphere and makes the demanding task of landing the airplane on a pitching, rolling carrier deck just that little bit easier. But the gaping nose intake is a positive menace to deck crews and constant vigilance is essential—being sucked into the engine can ruin your whole day. **Below** A-7E Corsair, side number 304, of VA-97 'Warhawks' in low visibility scheme tied down on the USS *Coral Sea* (CV-43) in July 1983. The pilots entry ladder is extended.
Overleaf A line-up of A-7Es aboard the USS *America* (CV-66) in July 1984. Side numbers 306/310 belong to VA-46 'Clansmen', and side numbers 410/401 belong to VA-72 'Blue Hawks'. SLUF translates into 'short little ugly fella' in polite company

A-7E of VA-83 'Rampages' equipped with a FLIR (forward-looking infrared) pod under its right wing is directed to one of *Saratoga*'s bow catapults. The Corsair can dangle an encyclopaedic variety of death and destruction under eight hardpoints spread under its wings and belly; Rockeyes, Snakeyes, Walleyes, CBUs, rocket pods etc—you call, it hauls

A-7E Corsair, side number 407, of VA-81
'Sunliners', looking good for the number three wire
on the rain swept deck of *Saratoga*. Landing lights
are aglow to help the LSO (landing signal officer)
monitor its approach in poor visibility

Jet blast deflector raised behind it, an A-7E of VA-81 'Sunliners' brings its TF41 engine up to 100 per cent prior to being launched from *Saratoga* in August 1984. The VF-74 Tomcat in the background, side number 200, is assigned to the commander of the carrier air wing (CAG)

VA-83 Corsair teamed with a KA-6D, the tanker version of the A-6 Intruder, on *Saratoga*'s flight deck. Air-to-air refuelling (AAR) is an integral part of flying operations; 'tanks' are used to extend the range or endurance of the fighters and attack aircraft, and to save a crew from an early bath if their airplane is losing too much gas as a result of combat damage, a technical glitch, or taking too many wave-offs in marginal weather with only 'bingo' fuel. Side number 523 is a US Marine Corps KA-6D operated by VMA(AW)-533 'Hawks'

Steam billowing from the bow cat, an A-7E is lined up for launch from *Nimitz*

VA-82 Corsair pilot goes around for some more approach practice after a 'touch and go' landing on the *Nimitz*. *Salt One*, the Grumman C-1A Trader in the foreground, was assigned to *Nimitz* as a COD (carrier on-board delivery) aircraft when this picture was taken in January 1983. The Trader can take-off without catapult assistance on the carrier's 4.5 acre flight deck. **Overleaf** Carrying a 'buddy' refuelling pod under its left wing, an A-7E gets a wave-off from the LSO and begins its bolter pattern for another attempt

Weathering of the low visibility paint scheme is exemplified by this A-7E of VA-97 'Warhawks'. The A-7E first flew on 25 November 1968 and deliveries began the following year. Unlike the earlier A-7A/B, the E-model is powered by an Allison TF41 (a license-built Rolls-Royce RB.168 Spey turbofan) which produces 15,000 lb (6804 kg) of thrust. Other differences are a 20 mm M61 Vulcan cannon and more advanced avionics; the A-7E was one of the first aircraft fitted with a HUD (head-up display) for the pilot. A total of 535 A-7Es were built and despite the advent of the multi-role F/A-18 Hornet, the Corsair will remain a front-line aircraft with the Navy well into the nineties

Incomplete national insignia and extended in-flight refuelling probe distinguish this A-7E of VA-12 'Kiss Of Death'. The Navy prefers to use the probe and drogue method of in-flight refuelling rather than the 'flying boom' system used by the Air Force. Side number 400 indicates that this A-7 is flown by the CAG commander

Newly-painted A-7E, side number 307, of VA-82 'Marauders' is the nearest Corsair in this line-up on *Nimitz* in January 1983

Right VA-83 Corsair about to hit *Saratoga*'s deck in the typically flat, no-flare landing attitude which gives you a better view of the real estate during the approach and puts all your rubber on the deck at the same time

Overleaf Mix of VA-82 Corsairs (nearest) and VA-86 'Sidewinders' with A-6Es of VA-35 'Black Panthers' in the middle aboard *Nimitz*

High-tech, low-level: Prowler and Intruder

Grumman EA-6B Prowler of the tactical electronic warfare squadron VAQ-136 'Gauntlets' embarked on the USS *Dwight D. Eisenhower* (CVN-69) in June 1982. The first EA-6B flew in May 1968 and its ALQ-99 jamming system has been progressively up-graded to stay ahead in the 'battle of the beams' and successfully neutralize or deceive enemy radars and communications

EA-6B Prowler, side number 610, of VAQ-130
'Zappers' mingles with a crowd of S-3As, an A-7E,
and the folded tail of an SH-3H aboard the USS
Forrestal (CV-59) in July 1981

The Prowlers bulged fin-tip contains part of its extensive suite of ECM/ESM equipment—most of it is slung in special pods under the wings and fuselage. VAQ-135 operated this example during *America*'s Mediterranean deployment in 1984. Part of the Principality of Monaco can be seen in the background

Overleaf Inside the hangar deck of Saratoga: Grumman A-6E Intruder, side number 500, of VMA(AW)-533 'Hawks' flown by the CAG commander is flanked by an EA-6B of VMAQ-2

A-6E Intruder, side number 511, of VA-196 'Main Battery', aboard the USS *Coral Sea* (CV-43) in July 1983. The Intruder is a subsonic two-seat all-weather attack aircraft which began its US Navy career in February 1963. Intruder squadrons proved outstandingly successful during the Vietnam war—deep penetration missions against the North (often at night) produced good bombing scores and the A-6 became popular with its crews because of its inherent survivability. An advanced version, the A-6F, is scheduled for delivery in 1989 and it will keep the type in service well into the 21st century. The current E-model first flew in November 1970 and it's powered by two ultra-reliable Pratt & Whitney J52-8B turbojets rated at 9300 lb (4218 kg) thrust which give it a maximum speed of 644 mph (1037 km/h) at sea level and a typical combat range of 1011 miles (1627 km)

A-6 bombardier/navigator of VA-35 'Black Panthers' gets his paperwork into shape before the pilot arrives

A-6E Intruder (buno 159570) of VA-196 parked on the *Coral Sea*. The bulbous nose radome houses a Norden APQ-148 multi-mode radar for simultaneous ground mapping, target identification, tracking and ranging

A-6E TRAM of VA-35 is manoeuvred for launch on *Nimitz*. Located in the mini-turret under the nose, TRAM (target recognition attack multisensor) incorporates FLIR (forward looking infrared) and a laser tracker/designator. The first A-6E TRAM flew in October 1974

VA-196 Intruders on the *Coral Sea* amid a tightly
packed bunch of airplanes in July 1983. An A-7E
Corsair of VA-27 'Royal Maces' is parked in the
foreground, with F-4N Phantoms of VF-154 'Black
Knights' (since re-equipped with the F-14 Tomcat)
in varying shades of squadron markings to the rear

EA-6B Prowler, side number 607, of VMAQ-2 'Playboys' moves slowly towards the parking lot after landing aboard *Saratoga*. The latest ICAP-2 standard Prowlers had recently entered service when this picture was taken in August 1984, fitted with a digital power management system to maximize their effectiveness against a cohesive range of frequency agile emitters. In addition to the pilot, three crew are needed to operate the system

Top left A weapons trolley carrying Zuni rocket pods waits in front of an A-6E of VA-65 'Tigers' in the hangar deck of IKE, June 1982. Drop tanks are stowed up near the ceiling to save space

A-6E TRAM of VMA(AW)-533 in low visibility gray waits with two bar attached on *Saratoga*. MERs (multiple ejector racks) are stacked on the weapons trolley in the foreground

Bottom left The hangar deck of *Nimitz*: A-6E Intruder, side number 604, of VA-35, is on the right next to an S-3A. VA-82 Corsair on the left is ready to go topside

KA-6D Intruder of VMA(AW)-533 parked near the fantail of *Saratoga* behind an S-3A and SH-3H

Right EA-6B Prowler of VMAQ-2 about to engage the first arrester wire on *Saratoga* for a textbook touchdown

Phantoms forever

The McDonnell Douglas F-4 Phantom II has been *the* fighter aircraft for more than a generation, the benchmark design by which all others in its class were judged—and most didn't even come close. It is extremely unlikely that any Western jet combat aircraft will overtake the 5201 production total racked up by the F-4 between 1958 and 1981, and none will ever match the kudos of flying in it. Even today, despite new high-tech hardware like the F-16, F/A-18 and Mirage 2000, it's so good that at least three major aerospace companies are working on advanced versions, two of which (by the Boeing Military Airplane Company and Israel Aircraft Industries) involve transplanting its trusty J79s with Pratt & Whitney PW1120 turbofans.

In 1985 only two US Navy squadrons, VF-151 'Fighting Vigilantes' and VF-161 'Chargers', regularly fly the Phantom from a carrier deck (USS *Midway*), but the aircraft is still a front-line fighter with shore based Navy units and a dozen other air arms around the world

Left F-4S Phantom of VF-74 'Be-Devilers' (now flying the F-14, see first chapter) being prepared for launch from the USS *Forrestal* (CV-59) in July 1981. The fairing on the intake is a radar warning receiver (RWR). The ultimate Navy Phantom, the F-4S is fitted with two-position wing slats to increase its manoeuvrability and a Westinghouse AN/AWG-10A radar with look-down/shoot-down capability. Installing 'smokeless' General Electric J79-GE-10B engines finally ended the 'follow the smoke and find the Phantom' jibes levelled at earlier Navy (and Air Force) versions. A total of 248 F-4Js were converted to F-4S standard

Left 'First in Phantoms' proclaims the fin of this F-4 from VF-74, and so they were. The 'Be-Devilers' received their Phantoms in July 1961 and completed carrier qualification trials on *Saratoga* in October that same year

Bottom left Detail of F-4N Phantom of VF-154 'Black Knights' aboard *Coral Sea* in July 1983

Below F-4S Phantom of VFMA-115 'Silver Eagles'—a US Marine Corps squadron. When this picture was taken in July 1981, VFMA-115 was assigned to *Forrestal*'s carrier air wing 17 (CVW-17) instead of the Navy F-4 unit VF-11 'Red Rippers'

Right Detail of F-4S Phantom of VF-74 in light gray scheme

Bottom right Detail of F-4N Phantom in low visibility gray showing extended in-flight refuelling probe and ECM antenna

This page and top right F-4N Phantom, side number 114, of VF-154 'Black Knights': its overall low visibility gray scheme and subdued national insignia give the aircraft a drab appearance—a complete contrast to the vivid, colourful Navy Phantoms of the sixties and seventies. The close-up below reveals that at least one of its intake guards has been borrowed from VF-21 'Freelancers'. Two drone 'kills' are stencilled on the intake splitter plate

Bottom right This VF-154 Phantom appears to have a form of wraparound camouflage under its left wing. The F-4N is a rebuild of the F-4B and features an improved structure, helmet-sight visual target acquisition system (VTAS), Sidewinder expanded acquisition mode (SEAM), a new main computer and one-way datalink. A total of 228 F-4B airframes were modified to F-4N standard

Staying with the subject of splitter plates, this F-4N of VF-21 'Freelancers' is wearing awards for excellence—'E' and safety—'S'

Right F-4N Phantoms of VF-154 (nearest) and VF-21 secured to the rear deck of *Coral Sea*. A crane has been swung out in the foreground

Defensive double act: Hawkeye and Viking

Left Taken from the island of *America,* an E-2C of VAW-123 'Cyclops' displays its artistic rotodome

An E-2C Hawkeye of VAW-124 'Bullseye Hummers' is catapulted from *Nimitz.* The pilot will fly a zig-zag pattern at low-level to prevent an enemy AEW aircraft detecting his departure and thus giving away the position of the carrier

Left This VAW-121 Hawkeye aboard IKE has its rotodome fully lowered so the aircraft will fit into the hangar deck. Before flight, hydraulics lift and lock the 2000 lb (910 kg) rotodome to maximize radar performance. **Bottom left** E-2C Hawkeye of VAW-125 'Torchbearers' tucks its wings away after landing aboard *Saratoga*. During flight operations the Hawkeye is the first fixed-wing aircraft to take-off and the last one to land. Normally the SH-3H rescue helicopter is the real early bird and only lands after the last aircraft has been safely recovered. **Right and below** E-2C Hawkeye of VAW-125 spreads its wings before being launched from *Saratoga*

Airborne early warning (AEW) is an absolutely critical part of a carrier's defences because even the most powerful surface radars can't see over the horizon. Without AEW, low-level strike aircraft can sneak in and cripple the carrier and other warships in the battle group with stand-off weapons such as sea-skimming anti-ship missiles (ASMs). Enter Hawkeye. The current E-2C 'Miniwacs' can detect fighters at ranges in excess of 200 nm (370 km), bombers at the limit of its (classified) radar range, cruise missiles at ranges in excess of 125 nm (231 km), and it's detected fast patrol boats (FPBs) at over 100 nm (185 km). The system can automatically track at least 600 targets simultaneously and take automatic control of more than 40 intercepts and strike missions.

The Hawkeye's AN/APS-125 radar is manufactured by General Electric, enclosed in a circular Randtron AN/APN-171 rotodome. Three crew (known as 'moles') operate the system: air controller to the rear, combat information officer in the middle, and a radar operator at the front. There isn't enough space to accommodate a relief crew, so after a typical four hour mission spent staring into display consoles in a dark, windowless compartment, the moles tap down their helmet

visors before stepping out into the sunlight, ready
to be led along the flight deck like little children
crossing a busy road. **Left** E-2C of VAW-125
'Torchbearers' taxies out for launch from *Saratoga*.
The E-2C is powered by two Allison T56-A-425
turboprops each rated at 4910 shp (3661 kW). Its
Hamilton Standard propellers employ glassfibre to
protect the radar from Doppler interference.
Above The previous model: an E-2B Hawkeye of
VAW-113 'Black Hawks' parked on the *Coral Sea*
in July 1983

Left Grumman C-1A Trader, *Salt One*, catches the wire and comes safely aboard the *Nimitz*. The Trader is a derivative of the Hawkeye's predecessor in the AEW role, the E-1B Tracer. It is powered by two Wright R-1820 radials each rated at 1525 hp (1138 kW)

Below Detail of a Lockheed S-3A Viking anti-submarine warfare (ASW) aircraft of VS-30 'Sea Tigers' aboard the *Forrestal* in July 1981. The S-3A first flew in 1972 and in addition to the dedicated ASW version Lockheed also built one KS-3A tanker and six US-3A COD aircraft

Bottom left The Trader's replacement, the Grumman C-2A Greyhound, began appearing on carrier decks in 1966. It has an obvious family resemblance to the Hawkeye but the fuselage is entirely new and can accommodate up to 39 passengers or 10,000 lb (4535 kg) of cargo. A C-2A from VR-24 is almost ready to be boosted from the deck of *Saratoga*

VS-30 Viking unfolds its wings and waits behind a jet blast deflector prior to being launched from one of *Forrestal*'s bow catapults. A VFMA-115 F-4S is lined-up on the other bow cat in the background. The Viking entered fleet service in 1974 and it replaced the Grumman S-2 Tracer. Like the Hawkeye, the Viking is a brilliant exercise in packaging an advanced weapons system into a relatively small airframe. Under a contract awarded to Lockheed in 1981 up to 160 Vikings are being updated to S-3B standard, introducing Harpoon anti-ship missile capability, a new sonobuoy reference system, better acoustic processing and enhanced electronic support measures (ESM). A retractable magnetic anomaly detector (MAD) is carried in the tail

Wings still folded, the pilot and co-pilot go through their check lists before cranking up the Vikings two 9280 lb (4210 kg) thrust General Electric TF34 turbofans. A tactical co-ordinator and a sensor operator sit in the aft cabin; all four crew have zero-zero ejection seats. The wing-tip pods house ESM antennae

Overleaf Leaving a cloud of steam behind it, a VS-30 Viking is catapulted against a dramatic sky from the *Saratoga* in August 1984. **Inset** GO! The catapult officer points the way for the S-3A

Above Looking for the second wire, an S-3A Viking, side number 707, of VS-30, prepares to trap aboard the *Saratoga*. **Right** The same airplane folding its wings; their high-aspect ratio design helps to give the Viking a sea level endurance of some 7.5 hours. When the aircraft has detected a submarine it can kill it with torpedoes and depth charges carried in an internal weapons bay or mounted on underwing pylons

Men at work

The flight deck of an aircraft carrier is no place for the faint hearted or work-shy. Side-stepping jet blast, the deadly suction of intakes, whirling propellers, busy tow tractors and ducking under the wings of launching aircraft either becomes instinctive or you become a statistic. On a deck with no railings—not even a handhold—positional awareness and good judgement is essential. At every level of flying operations safety is a way of life. **Left** Ordnance men: the colour of a deck crewman's jersey, life jacket, and helmet tells everyone around him what kind of job he does. **Overleaf** EA-6B Prowler of VAQ-130 'Zappers' on the *Forrestal* with a rapid intervention fire vehicle in attendance

Each squadron on a carrier has its own landing signal officer (LSO), a veteran pilot who guides his fellow aviators down the approach. If a pilot is flying his airplane nicely on the glideslope and sticking to the centreline, the LSO will mainly confine his patter to reassurance. If a pilot isn't getting it right, the LSO will feed him corrections and sort things out; if the pilot really screws up, or if the deck becomes obstructed, the LSO will give him a wave-off and send him around again

Two hook-up men inspect one of the arrester
cables on *Forrestal*. They prepare aircraft for launch
and secure them to the catapults

A 'mule' driver takes five on the *Saratoga*. Mules are yellow tractors used to move airplanes on the flight and hangar decks. A blue jacket with a stencilled 'T' entitles you to drive your own machine and enjoy the luxury of being able to sit down most of the time

Right When the catapult officer drops his knee and points down the deck, the 'shooter' presses a button which signals the order to fire to the catapult controller a deck below

Left *Nimitz'* Oshkosh fire truck stands by in front of the island. **Above** Firemen relax on the roof of a different fire truck on *Forrestal*

Right A tow tractor (short variety) with a load of wheel chocks

Overleaf The next job for this tow tractor is to haul away the Prowler parked in the background

The cockpit of tow tractor number 14: a rough anti-slip coating decorates the top of the vehicle

A mule on the move. In addition to their towing
tasks, the larger tractors like this one can carry a
generator on the back for starting aircraft

F-14 Tomcat of VF-41 'Black Aces' in an experimental low visibility scheme ready to be towed away on the *Nimitz* in January 1983

Left Ordnance men with the ammunition loading system they use to feed shells into the magazine of the Vulcan M61 rotary cannon used by the A-7 and F-14. These men also handle and load bombs, missiles, torpedoes, sensors and jammers

Right Aircraft are refuelled by 'grapes'—men wearing purple jackets. A Corsair is receiving its fill of JP5 through the pressure hose plugged in near the landing gear. The airplane is carrying an AIM-9L Sidewinder (fitted with its protective nose cap) on its left-hand missile rail

Far left Refuelling an F-14 Tomcat

Left Green-shirted maintenance men peer under an unlatched access panel on a Tomcat prior to fixing a minor avionics problem

Below Two F-14 Tomcats of VF-84 'Jolly Rogers' on the *Nimitz*. The airplane on the left is ready to be towed out; the plane captain in the front cockpit is there to work the toe brakes as the aircraft makes its way across the deck. Every airplane in the air wing has a plane captain (identified by his brown jacket) who is responsible for ensuring the serviceability and cleanliness of the machine under his charge

Overleaf A RIO climbs into the rear cockpit of a VF-74 Tomcat

Above A plane captain inspects the rear Martin-Baker GRU-7A ejection seat of a Tomcat during a serviceability check

Left Sorting out the 'black boxes' in an A-7E

Right Armed with practice bombs, an A-6E Intruder of VA-35 'Black Panthers' needs a firm shove to get it into the right spot before starting up

Overleaf A maintenance man perched on the tail section of a Sikorsky SH-3H Sea King helicopter of HS-3 'Tridents' aboard *Saratoga*

The crew of an SH-3H rescue helicopter walk towards their machine across the rainy deck of *Saratoga*. Its rotor blades and tail are still folded

Right Agility is a quality common to many maintenance men, but working on helicopters can be especially demanding. This Sea King, and the one next to it, belong to HS-9 'Sea Griffins' on *Nimitz*

Overleaf Boeing Vertol CH-46D Sea Knight of HC-6 (Detachment 6) from the USS *Seattle* (AOE-3) lands to deliver mail to the crew of *Saratoga*

While IKE rides at anchor off Monaco, a KA-6D Intruder of VA-65 'Tigers' is washed down to protect its aluminium airframe from the effects of salt corrosion

Scrubbing the decks is probably the oldest naval tradition, bit it's just as important today—after a sustained period of flight operations the deck becomes slick with vented jet fuel, lubricants, and hydraulic fluid

In port

Left and overleaf The USS *America* was commissioned in January 1965 and in common with the other three Kitty Hawk class carriers she is powered by four Westinghouse steam turbines with a combined output of 280,000 shp (208,955 kW), giving a maximum speed of 33 knots (61 km/h). The ship displaces 80,800 tons and is crewed by 5380 men

Preceding page The USS *Coral Sea* anchored in the Bay of Cannes in July 1983. Commissioned in October 1947, an extensive modification programme included the installation of an angled flight deck, three steam-driven catapults, and the relocation of her elevators. Crewed by 4560 men, *Coral Sea* displaces 64,000 tons and is powered by four Westinghouse steam turbines with a total output of 212,000 shp (158,208 kW), giving a maximum speed of 32 knots (59 km/h)

Above and right The Nimitz class carrier USS *Dwight D. Eisenhower* is armed with approximately 95 aircraft and about half of them, gathered like nesting sea birds, are parked on the flight deck in these views of the carrier in the picturesque Bay of Monaco

F-14 Tomcat of VF-33 'Tarsiers' parked near the fantail of *America* with the hilly terrain of Naples in the background

Douglas EA-3B Skywarrior of the fleet air reconnaissance squadron VQ-2 remained aboard IKE when the carrier visited Monaco in June 1982. The Skywarrior is nicknamed 'The Whale' because of its shape and size

Overleaf and following pages The vast bulk of the *Dwight D. Eisenhower* on display in the port of Athens in March 1982: the carrier has an overall length of 1092 ft (332.8 m) and a maximum beam of 252 ft (76.8 m); full displacement is 93,405 tons. Its two Westinghouse A4W pressurized water nuclear reactors can generate a total of 280,000 shp (208,955 kW) and give the carrier unlimited range and a maximum speed of at least 32 knots (59 km/h). Of its total complement of 6280, 2620 are aviation personnel